# LEGENDS OF WARFARE
## GROUND

# Sherman Tank, Vol. 3
America's M4A2 Medium Tank in World War II

**DAVID DOYLE**

SCHIFFER MILITARY
4880 Lower Valley Road   Atglen, PA 19310

Designed by Justin Watkinson
Type set in Impact/Minion Pro/Univers LT Std
Front cover photo by John Blackman

ISBN: 978-0-7643-6092-3
Printed in China

Published by Schiffer Publishing, Ltd.
4880 Lower Valley Road
Atglen, PA 19310
Phone: (610) 593-1777; Fax: (610) 593-2002
E-mail: Info@schifferbooks.com
www.schifferbooks.com

For our complete selection of fine books on this and related subjects, please visit our website at www.schifferbooks.com. You may also write for a free catalog.

Schiffer Publishing's titles are available at special discounts for bulk purchases for sales promotions or premiums. Special editions, including personalized covers, corporate imprints, and excerpts, can be created in large quantities for special needs. For more information, contact the publisher.

We are always looking for people to write books on new and related subjects. If you have an idea for a book, please contact us at proposals@schifferbooks.com.

# Acknowledgments

This book would not have been possible without the gracious help of many individuals and institutions. Beyond the invaluable help provided by the staffs of the National Archives and the Patton Museum, I am deeply indebted to Tom Kailbourn, Scott Taylor, Steve Zaloga, Dana Bell, Jim Gilmore, General Motors LLC, John Blackman, Chris Hughes, Joe DeMarco, Kurt Laughlin, and Pat Stansell. Their generous and skillful assistance adds immensely to the quality of this volume. In addition to such wonderful friends and colleagues, the Lord has blessed me with a wonderful wife, Denise, who has tirelessly scanned thousands of photos and documents for this and numerous other books. Beyond that, she is an ongoing source of support and inspiration.

# Contents

# Introduction

The series of medium tanks known as the M4 Sherman constituted the backbone of the US armored force during World War II. In addition, Sherman tanks made up a major portion of the armored forces of America's allies in the first years after the Second World War. Nearly 50,000 Shermans rolled off assembly lines during World War II, a number that dwarfs the figures for total German panzer output from 1939 to 1945.

The deteriorating global situation toward the end of the 1930s propelled the development of the M4A2 and the whole M4 tank series. In August 1940, the US Army Ordnance Department issued a contract for the manufacture of 1,000 medium tanks of the M2A1 type. To facilitate this production, Chrysler received a contract to operate the Detroit Arsenal Tank Plant, which at that date was yet to be constructed. Yet, even as these contracts were being issued, panzer divisions were leading German forces to victory after victory in Europe. France, previously thought the most powerful state on the Continent, quickly collapsed before the Blitzkrieg onslaught of "Schneller Heinz" Guderian's panzers. Compared to contemporaneous German armor, America's M2A1 was demonstrably obsolete even before the Detroit plant had been built. Accordingly, the Rock Island Arsenal, in the end, turned out the few M2A1 tanks that were constructed (and were later used as training vehicles), while the new Detroit facility was directed toward manufacture of the M3 medium tank—yet another interim vehicle.

Although it was an improvement over the M2A1, the M3 (or "General Lee," as it would come to be known) still suffered from a number of flaws. The M3's 75 mm gun was fitted in a sponson that could traverse only within a limited range, while the turret in which the Lee's secondary 37 mm antitank gun was mounted could rotate a full 360 degrees. This anomaly was due to the fact that no producible design for a proper main-gun turret had yet been produced. More generally, the M3's riveted construction was another shortcoming, as was the vehicle's tall, vulnerable silhouette (a feature partly due to the M3's radial engine).

Over the course of production, some of the General Lee's inadequacies were corrected. Welded-hull and cast-hull variants of the M3 were developed, eliminating the rivets that would ricochet like bullets around the hull interior when the vehicle sustained a hit.

Nevertheless, the General Lee was not a total failure. The vehicle's drivetrain and suspension functioned well, and its 75 mm main gun gave the British and American forces much-needed firepower on the North African front.

No less important was the fact that through their participation in the M3 program, the makers of the M3 medium tank—Detroit Tank Arsenal, American Locomotive Company, Baldwin Locomotive Works, Pullman-Standard Car Company, and Pressed Steel Car Company—gained invaluable experience in tank manufacture, which paved the way to the successful introduction of the M4 series.

A solution for turret-mounting the 75 mm gun appeared to have been found by February 1941, when a mockup of a new design for a new medium tank started to come together at the Aberdeen Proving Ground. Featuring the lower hull, suspension, and drivetrain of the M3, the new tank was designated the T6. The T6 incorporated a 69-inch turret ring and a front plate that was removable, so as to facilitate removal of the 75 mm gun. The operational pilot model of the T6 was completed at Aberdeen by September 1 of that year, just six months after completion of the M3 pilot.

The first model produced of the M4 series of medium tanks was the Medium Tank M4A1, which featured a cast-armor upper hull. Early M4A1s had bogie assemblies similar to those of the Medium Tank M3 Lee/Grant, and direct-vision ports were supplied for the driver and the assistant driver, to the fronts of their hatches. Pictured here is the second M4A1, which bore the nickname "MICHAEL" on placards on the sponsons, in tribute to Michael Dewar, chief of the British Tank Mission to the United States.

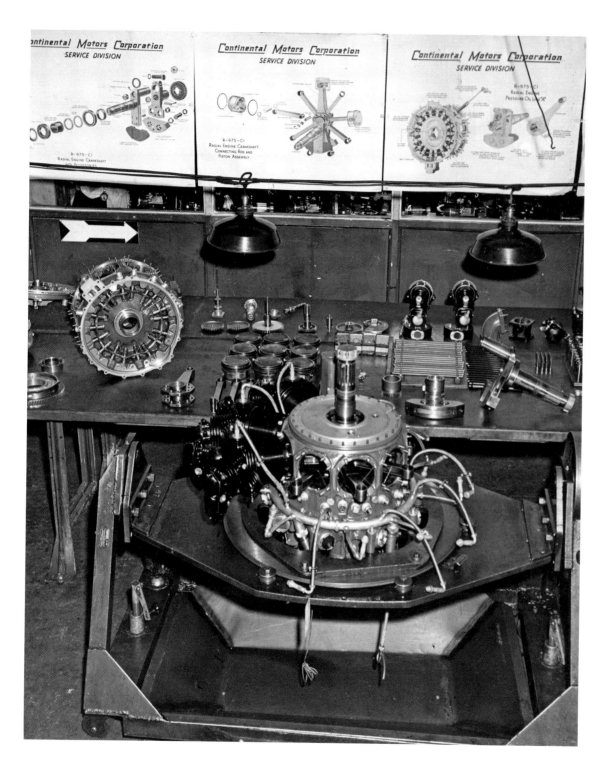

The power plant of the M4A1 was the Wright R-975-C1 Whirlwind radial engine, also built under license by Continental Motors Corporation. This nine-cylinder radial engine had a displacement of 973 cubic inches and a maximum of 400 net horsepower at 2,400 rpm. During World War II, Continental Motors mounted this exhibition of a partially disassembled Whirlwind along with a table full of engine parts and a number of posters showing the workings of the engine. *Jim Gilmore collection*

A Continental R-975 Whirlwind engine is viewed from the left rear in a photo dated March 16, 1942. Around the rears of the cylinders is the exhaust manifold. Fuel and oil lines are installed, but the electric starter, which fit above and between the two magnetos on the center rear of the engine, has not been mounted. *National Archives*

The Medium Tank M4, featuring a welded hull, would seem to have preceded the Medium Tank M4A2 on the basis of their alphanumeric designations, but the M4A2 beat the M4 into production by almost three months, with Fisher Tank Arsenal and Pullman-Standard Car Company commencing production of that model in April 1942. Like the M4A1, the M4 was powered by the Wright/Continental R-975-C1 engine. The M4 shown here is the small-hatch, direct-vision type and is thought to have been produced by Pressed Steel Car. *National Archives*

# CHAPTER 1

# M4A2 Dry Stowage, Direct Vision

As seen in an Aberdeen Proving Ground photo dated April 22, 1942, Medium Tank M4A2, registration number W-3014311 and Ordnance number 2305, was the first tank of that model produced by Fisher Tank Arsenal to be accepted by the Army. Initially, in addition to the assistant driver's flexible, ball-mounted .30-caliber bow machine gun, this model had two extra .30-caliber machine guns in the bow, but soon these were discontinued. *Patton Museum*

The first welded-hull Sherman tank to enter production was the M4A2. Beating out the M4 by a few months, the M4A2 began production at Fisher Tank Arsenal and Pullman-Standard Car Company in April 1942. In September 1943, American Locomotive Company added its name to the list of firms manufacturing the M4A2. Then Baldwin Locomotive Works came onboard in October, and Federal Machine and Welder joined the manufacturers in November 1943.

The M4A2 incorporated an engine deck that was significantly different from that of the M4. The two diesel engines of the M4A2 required a bigger air inlet grille on the vehicle's forward plate. Bracketing the grille were four filler caps, which remain today the simplest way to identify the M4A2. Welded around each of the four caps was a metal label that identified the purpose of the reservoir under the cap. The labels for the two forward caps were marked "LUBRICATING OIL," and the two rear labels read "WATER." Additional outside caps were designated "Diesel FUEL OIL."

The air inlet grilles that dominated the plate were each held in place by two bolts. Each fitted with a lift handle, both the grille panels swung outward on hinges. Bolted on to the front edge of the engine deck was a splash guard that covered the rear of the turret race, guarding it against damage. Bolted to the sides of the engine compartment were the two side deck panels that incorporated the water and oil filler caps.

In contrast to the configuration of the M4 and M4A1, the rear engine deck plate on the M4A2 extended all the way to the rear hull plate. Although in most respects similar to the rear hull plate on early M4 tanks, the M4A2 rear hull plate was sloped.

Unique among Sherman tanks was the M4A2's exhaust system. With two big resonance chambers, the M4A2 exhaust system is readily identifiable. No exhaust deflectors were present on the very first of the production models of the tank.

The early-production M4A2s had direct-vision ports and small hatches for the driver and the assistant driver and were fitted with three-piece, bolted final-drive assemblies. The small hatches are open, showing the periscopes on swiveling mounts on them. The early M4A2s were classified as "dry-stowage" tanks, insofar as their 75 mm ammunition was stowed without being surrounded by a solution of water and antifreeze, to limit the damage should an incoming projectile strike and detonate the ammunition. *Patton Museum*

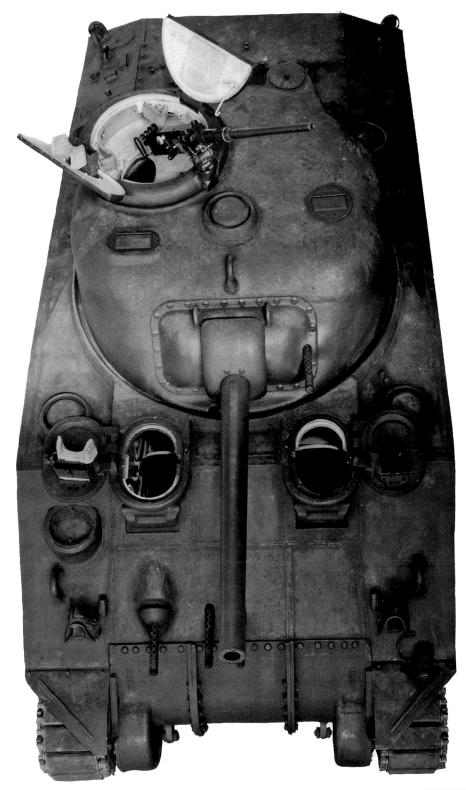

As seen on registration number W-3014311, unlike the welded-hull Medium Tank M4, the M4A2 had a taller rear plate for the upper hull. Two holders are on that plate for securing the idler-adjusting wrench. Below the turret bustle, at the front of the engine deck, is bolted a splash guard, which was fabricated at the Fisher plant. Other features such as the pistol port on the left side of the turret and the mudguards on the rear of the upper hull are in view. Barely visible below the rear plate of the upper hull are the two mufflers and the exhausts. *Patton Museum*

As seen in a right-side view of this M4A2, registration number W-3014311, the slope of the glacis on the direct-vision, dry-stowage vehicles was 57 degrees from vertical. The M4A2 technical manual referred to this style of bogie assemblies, with the track-support rollers centered over the bogie brackets (sometimes called bogie frames), as the "first type suspensions." *Patton Museum*

The purpose of the enlarged rear armor plate on the upper hull was to protect the radiator, which was between the rear of the power plant and this plate. Whereas the Wright/Continental Whirlwind engines that powered the Medium Tanks M4A1 and M4 were air-cooled, the M4A2 was equipped with the water-cooled General Motors 6046 engine. *Patton Museum*

The engine deck of the M4A2 varied significantly from those of the M4 and M4A1 medium tanks. It was fitted with two grille/doors, with two hinges on the outboard sides of each unit. To the forward sides of the grille/doors were six armored covers for fillers, three per side. The outboard fillers were for diesel fuel, the front inboard filler was for lubricating oil, and the rear inboard filler was for engine coolant. Also in view is the commander's split hatch, with a rotating hatch ring equipped with a mount for a Browning .50-caliber M2 HB antiaircraft machine gun. A periscope on a rotating mount was on one of the hatch doors.
*Patton Museum*

A General Motors 6046 engine, the power plant for the M4A2, is viewed from the left front. The 6046 engine was composed of two GM 6-71 diesel engines, which fed their output via flywheels to a double-clutch housing and a power transfer unit, which then transferred output to the driveshaft, often called the propeller shaft. *General Motors LLC*

The output end of the GM 6046 engine is viewed from straight ahead, showing, at the bottom, the transfer gear case, at the center of which is the connection for the universal joint and the driveshaft. Above and to the rear of the transfer case are the two engine blocks and the valve covers. *General Motors LLC*

In a right-front view of the 6046 engine, the mounts for the two generators, which aren't installed, are on the outer fronts of the engine blocks, just above the transfer case. Six-pointed covers are screwed over the mountings for the generators. The bullet-shaped object on the lower rear side of the engine block is the right engine-oil strainer. The black object to the front of the strainer is the Delco-Remy starting motor and solenoid. *General Motors LLC*

As seen from the right side of the 6046 engine, the tapered object on the side of the engine block is the air inlet housing; on top of it are three bright-metal mountings for three separate air cleaners. Alongside the rear of the engine block, adjacent to the rear of the valve cover, is an AC KleerKleen fuel oil filter. *General Motors LLC*

The left side of the 6046 engine is the mirror image of the right side, complete with air-inlet housing, engine starter and solenoid, engine-oil strainer, fuel filter, and so forth. Each half of the 6046 engine had its own electrical, lubricating, cooling, and fuel systems, so that if one half of the engine failed, the other half could continue operating. *General Motors LLC*

A GM 6046 engine is observed from the rear end, which the engine's technical manual referred to as the fan end. The elbows with light-toned faces at the top of the engine are the fan drives. The two wheel-shaped features near the bottom of the engine are vibration dampers. The two inverted elbows between the fan drives were the exhaust-manifold elbows. *General Motors LLC*

ORDNANCE OPERATIO
GENERAL MOTORS
PROVING GROUND
PROJECT 27
MEDIUM TANK
M4A2

3·4 FRONT VIEW
PG 8019
MAY 9 1942 NEG A

American Locomotive Company (ALCO), of Schenectady, New York, was another manufacturer of M4A2s. This example was photographed during testing by the Ordnance Operation, General Motors Proving Ground, on May 9, 1942. The glacis was formed from multiple panels of plate armor that were welded together. At the top of the glacis are two hoods, which held the driver's and assistant driver's hatch doors on top and the direct-vision port covers on the fronts. The cylindrical feature jutting from the right side of the glacis was a radio antenna bracket. *Patton Museum*

ORDNANCE OPERATION
GENERAL MOTORS
PROVING GROUND
PROJECT 27
MEDIUM TANK
M4A2

3-4   REAR   VIEW
PG 8019
MAY 9 1942  NEG A80

The ALCO M4A2 is observed from the left rear. A first-type suspension was installed on this chassis. The object near the rear of the engine deck is a temporary piece of equipment: a rectangle of plywood with three bullet-shaped objects on top, possibly lights. An electrical wire leads from a hole in the engine deck to this fixture. Prior to shipping this tank from the factory, workers had applied sealant tape over the pistol port on the turret and on other joints where moisture might infiltrate, and much of this tape was still present on the tank when it was photographed. *Patton Museum*

The same ALCO M4A2 is seen from above during evaluations at the General Motors Proving Ground on May 9, 1942. Note the diagonal positioning of the two grab handles on the rear parts of the grille/doors for engine intake air. Sealing tape is over the openings for the periscopes on the turret roof, hatch, ventilator, and antenna bracket, as well as on the 75 mm gun shield and other locations. The periscope rotors have been removed from the driver's and assistant driver's hatches. *Patton Museum*

A final photo of the M4A2 under evaluation at the GM Proving Ground shows the engine with the grille/doors open; the view is facing forward. At the top are the four lubricating oil filters, flanked on each side by a fuel filter. Between the valve covers are the exhaust manifolds. Two air-bleeder-valve knobs are at the bottom of the photo. *Patton Museum*

The US Army Armor & Cavalry Collection, Fort Benning, Georgia, preserves the first M4A2 medium tank produced by American Locomotive Company, Ordnance number 1405, and accepted in September 1942. Mounted on the chassis is a Sherman Firefly turret armed with a 17-pounder gun. The British sent this turret to the United States for evaluation by the Army Ground Forces Board and the Ordnance Department during the latter part of World War II, and apparently it was mounted on this M4A2 chassis after the war, replacing the original D50878 75mm turret.

The bogie assemblies on the chassis of this M4A2, Ordnance number 1405, replaced the first-type suspension and was one of a number of similar designs collectively referred to as part number D47527. These particular bogie units feature bogie brackets (sometimes called bogie frames) with a horizontal mold seam near the top and are equipped with the final-design skids on the tops of the bogie brackets, with rounded fronts and straight, angled rears.

In a left-rear view of M4A2, Ordnance number 1405, note the small openings on the splash guards around the turret and the fuel filler, to prevent water from being trapped behind the guards.

On the front of the engine deck, below the turret bustle, is the rear section of the turret splash guard. The light-colored patterns on this guard are indentations to provide clearance for the bolts that secure the guard to the deck.

Atop the right sponson are holders for pioneer tools (not present here), including a shovel, ax, mattock head and handle, and crowbar.

The rounded hump to the inboard side of the bow machine gun was a feature found on a few early M4A2s. On the inboard side of each brush guard is a tube, which was used for storing a plug that was inserted in the headlight socket when the headlight assemblies were removed from the glacis

This M4A2, Ordnance number 1405, originally was shipped to Aberdeen Proving Ground with a single-piece final-drive assembly installed. The three-piece final-drive assembly now on the tank was salvaged from the first Pacific Car and Foundry M4A1 at Aberdeen Proving Ground. The driver's direct-vision port cover is partly open, while the assistant driver's is closed.

The driver's direct-vision port cover is seen from the front. The front of the cover is flat and quite smooth, with curved machining marks lightly etched on it.

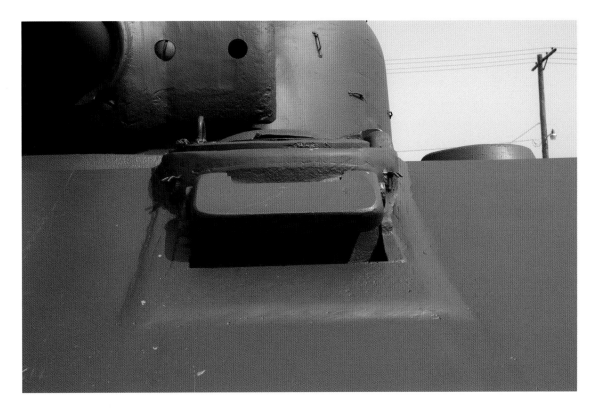

The driver's hood, the partially open direct-vision port cover, and the hinge for the hatch door are viewed close-up from the left side. Also of interest are the casting marks on the rounded part of the gun shield.

Details of the left side of the Sherman Firefly turret on M4A2, Ordnance number 1405, are displayed, including the pistol port, the left lifting ring, and the armored box mounted on the turret bustle to contain the wireless (radio) set.

A final image of American Locomotive–built M4A2, Ordnance number 1405, focuses on the three armored covers for fluid fillers, as seen from the right side of the tank. In the foreground is the cover for the right fuel filler. The other two covers are for engine oil (*right*) and coolant (*left*). Metal, embossed labels are tack-welded to the hull, next to the covers for the oil and coolant fillers, identifying their purposes. Also in view to the right is the grille/door for engine-air intake and the rear of the splash guard for the turret, showing the indentations for the bolts that fasten the guard to the deck.

Baldwin Locomotive was a minor producer of M4A2s, completing just twelve examples in October and November 1942. The final Baldwin M4A2, registration number 3010770 and Ordnance serial number 1916, as displayed here, was a small-hatch, direct-vision type, completed in November 1942. Visible on the side of the turret in raised figures is its serial number, 1565. The rotor shield, or mantlet, for the 75 mm gun was the early type, which did not extend to the sides as the later types did. The port for the coaxial machine gun is taped over. *Baldwin Locomotive Works*

The fairing for the bow machine gun on the Baldwin Locomotive M4A2s had a flat face with a sharp edge around it; this feature is visible here and in the preceding photo. The lifting rings on the glacis were the so-called "bent rod" type, with circular cross sections. The direct-vision port covers had the name of their manufacturer, Stockham, in raised letters on their fronts; the assistant driver's port cover also had the number 230 on it. The glacis was a weldment of six armor panels (counting the two drivers' hood castings). *Baldwin Locomotive Works*

With the tracks of the Baldwin M4A2 pulled up on a curb, details of the lower part of the single-piece final-drive assembly are discernible. Faintly visible on the bottom of the final-drive assembly is the "SS" trademark of its maker, the Scullin Steel Company, St. Louis, Missouri. T41 tracks are installed. *Baldwin Locomotive Works*

# CHAPTER 2
# Dry Stowage, Periscope Vision

Federal Machine and Welder Company (FMW), of Warren, Ohio, was another builder of M4A2s, completing 540 examples. The direct-vision ports were eliminated on this dry-stowage vehicle, replaced in both positions by a new hood with a periscope on the top front. An angle iron was welded laterally across the glacis between the hoods as a handgrip/step. Partially surrounding the bow machine gun mount is a tubular structure with snap fittings on it, for attaching a dustcover for that gun. *National Archives*

Initial-production M4A2 tanks featured vision slits located directly in front of the driver and codriver. This configuration has earned those early vehicles the designation "direct-vision tanks." Although armored doors protected the vision slits, it later became evident that the area of the slits was particularly vulnerable. Little gaps around the protective visors permitted fragments of bullets and shells into the tank's fighting compartment, inflicting casualties among the crew members and threatening detonation of ammunition. Accordingly, the direct-vision doors were eliminated from the casting of the hull in late 1942. Still, though, the hatches for the driver and codriver remained rectangular in shape and mounted on a hinge that ran parallel to the side of the hull, as they had been on the direct-vision M4A2. All the Shermans with this hatch configuration are now referred to as "small-hatch" tanks.

Engineers with Fisher Tank Arsenal set out to remedy the vulnerability of the area of the vision slits. Keen not to have to rely on outside supply for the parts, they designed box-shaped structures, dubbed "hoods" by many, that could replace the direct-vision features. The welded hoods, which replaced the direct-vision assembly in the last quarter of 1942, gave M4A2 vehicles from Fisher Tank Arsenal a unique, easily spotted appearance.

At nearly the same time, a new, heavy-duty vertical-volute suspension system (VVSS), designated D47527, was also introduced. While on the older D37892 suspension the return roller was mounted directly over the center of the suspension unit, on the D47527 more space was allotted for larger springs within the bogie. This arrangement made for better handling of the tank's weight.

Also introduced was a single-piece cast housing for the differential and final-drive assembly. With its greater rigidity and therefore enhanced reliability, the one-piece E4186 started to take the place of the earlier three-piece design. Engineers from Ford Motor Company took credit for this design.

Another modification to the tank, one less apparent than the modifications noted above, was the addition to the roof of the turret of a blade sight ahead of the commander to help him traverse the turret rapidly in order to lay the gun on a target. "Ears" were added to the outer rotor shield casting of the M34 gun mount. These features served to protect the gun barrel's recoil area from small-arms fire. Eventually a new gun mount, designated M34A1, replaced the M34. The M34A1 featured a wider shield that included a direct-vision telescopic gunsight. The shield also afforded protection for the coaxial machine gun.

The now-familiar diesel-pattern engine deck was a feature of the vehicle, though another cap appeared on the rear deck plate as a result of a change in the engine oil system in order to decrease dirt contamination and improve cooling. The new cap, which had a label that read "ENGINE OIL GAUGE," allowed access to a rod for measuring fluid level. A label reading "GAS-OIL 30-1" was by now present on the auxiliary generator filler cap.

Fisher-built M4A2 tanks were used extensively by the US Marine Corps, and arguably the tank's most famous photograph recorded the vehicle's debut at Tarawa. The M4A2 remained in Marine service until it was replaced by the M4A2 with a large hatch, or by the M4A3. British, French, and Soviet forces received the small-hatch version of the M4A2.

This small-hatch, dry-stowage M4A2, in the collection of Gavin Copeman, in the UK, has been restored to running condition, currently operating under the nickname "BIG 0." In the tradition of World War II Shermans, a wooden plank between the mudguards serves as a retainer for gear stored on the glacis. Replica markings for the fifth vehicle of Company B, 66th Armored Regiment, 2nd Armored Division, are on the final-drive assembly. *John Blackman*

This vehicle has the "economy" type of D47366 sprockets, which lacked the intricate cutouts around the inner perimeter that earlier models of the D47366 sprockets had. The bogie wheels are the stamped, open-spoke C851643 model. The track-return rollers are mounted on spacers, to give them a bit more height. *John Blackman*

The tracks on this M4A2 are the T49 model, a steel, parallel-grouser design, with one long grouser and two short ones per link. This type of track was often used on US Marine Corps M4A2s in the Pacific theater. *John Blackman*

Details of the right fender, service headlight and blackout marker lamp combination, brush guard, lifting ring, antenna bracket, and assistant driver's hood are displayed. A casting number is present on the lower part of the flange of the antenna bracket. *John Blackman*

The driver's hood is shown close-up, with the periscope head protruding below its sprung lid. This design of driver's hood is called the narrow type; it was used on small-hatch M4s and M4A2s and has a subtle taper on its front, growing narrower toward the top. Seven weld beads were used to secure this hood to the glacis. *John Blackman*

Piggybacked on the service headlights—the left one is depicted—are blackout marker lamps. The brush guards were fabricated from welded steel strapping. The lifting rings are a type with a circular cross section, flared at the bottoms. *John Blackman*

The rotor shield, also called the mantlet, as seen from the right, is the E5721 type, which extended to both sides to give better protection to the gun shield: the armored front of the gun mount, which was screwed to the turret. This rotor shield was part of the Gun Mount M34A1. On the near side of the rotor shield is the port for the gunner's direct sight. On the opposite side is the coaxial machine-gun port. Note the two lifting rings welded to the upper part of the gun shield. *John Blackman*

The right side of the turret has pockmarks, evidently from machine gun and small-arms fire. On the front of the roof is a vane sight, which the commander used to quickly align the turret with a target. Beyond the vane sight is the cradle for a .50-caliber antiaircraft machine gun. Note the open flap for the periscope on the split hatch door. *John Blackman*

The turret bustle is observed from the left side of the tank, including the two antenna brackets on the rear of the roof. The W-in-C trademark of the Continental Foundry and Machine Company, Wheeling, West Virginia, is on the rear of the bustle. Note the style of the bolt-on section of splash guard below the bustle. *John Blackman*

A left-rear view of the turret bustle focuses on the pistol port and lifting ring. The hinged cover of the pistol port rests inside a splash guard built into the side of the turret. The splash guard acted to deflect bullets and splinters. Below the turret bustle, the hooded feature visible behind a notch in the turret splash guard is the housing for the pull handles for the fixed fire-extinguisher system. *John Blackman*

The driver's hood and hatch are viewed from above. The hatch cover or door has a bulge on top to give the driver a little extra headroom. To the front of the bulge is a sprung lid for a rotating periscope, and another, fixed periscope is on the front top of the hood. On the hatch door is its part number, D50884. On the top rear of the driver's hood assembly are casting marks, including the trademark of the American Steel Foundries, Granite City, Indiana, and the part number, D77160B. *John Blackman*

The assistant driver's hood has a slightly different part number than the driver's hood: D77160A. To the outboard side of the hood are, *left*, the antenna bracket, with a likely postwar plug welded on top of it, and, *right*, a ventilator, with—evidently—weld beads between the ventilator hood and the splash guard to eliminate the water trap. The small-hatch doors on this tank were an early type, lacking brush guards for the periscopes and equilibrator springs. *John Blackman*

In a view of the driver's compartment of the Copeman M4A2, the driver's hood and fixed M6 periscope are at the top. Below the periscope are the grips of the steering-brake levers, to the right of which is a small panel with three knobs; the top two are the clutch lockouts, and the lower one is the hand-throttle locking lever. Below this panel are the two hand-throttle levers. To the right is the transmission; above the floor are the accelerator pedal (*right*) and the clutch pedal (*left*). On the side wall of the lower hull is a periscope holder. To the right of the driver's seat is the gearshift lever. *John Blackman*

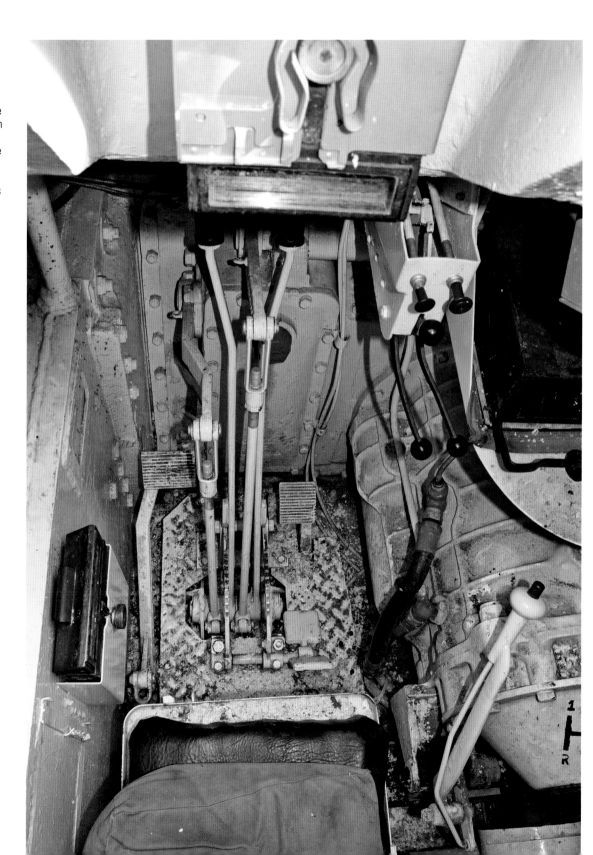

The driver's compartment is viewed more to the right, showing the transmission, the gearshift lever, the forward end of the driveshaft and its housing (*lower right*), and the assistant driver's seat (*upper right*). The rounded shelf above the transmission was used for storing the driver's foul-weather hood and four spare periscopes. *John Blackman*

The assistant driver's compartment is observed from above, with the seat to the left, the transmission to the top, and the fixed periscope, a .30-caliber ammunition box and holder, and a spare periscope and holder to the lower right. The red cap at the center of the photo is for the power-train lubricating-oil filler. *John Blackman*

The assistant driver's small-hatch door is open, showing the rotating mount for an M6 periscope and the bulge to provide extra headroom. On the hood to the front of the hatch is the hinged cover for the fixed M6 periscope. *John Blackman*

The front of the turret and the driver's and assistant driver's hoods and hatches, as well as the glacis, are viewed from atop the turret. On the rotor shield to each side of the 75 mm gun barrel are cast-in "cheeks," to protect the junction of the barrel and the shield. Between the two lifting eyes of the gun shield is the forward lifting eye of the turret. To the lower left are the front end of a vane sight and part of the .50-caliber antiaircraft gun cradle. *John Blackman*

The hatch ring (called the race assembly in the M4A2 ordnance supply catalog) on the turret is viewed from the rear; the commander's M6 periscope is on the hatch door to the right. To the front of the hatch is the roof ventilator and surrounding splash guard; note the two holes on the bottom of the guard to allow water to escape. Inside the hatch is the gunner's station. *John Blackman*

This is the gunner's view in the right side of the turret. To the left are the breech of the 75 mm gun and the white-painted recoil guard. Toward the top are the gunner's telescopic sight and the gunner's periscope. The white mechanism below the periscope is the elevating handwheel and gearbox, to the right of which is the manual traversing handwheel, with a vertical brass handle. Below the elevating handwheel is the hydraulic traversing mechanism, which includes, *left to right*, the hydraulic oil reservoir, the motor, the black traversing control handle, and a gray switch box. *John Blackman*

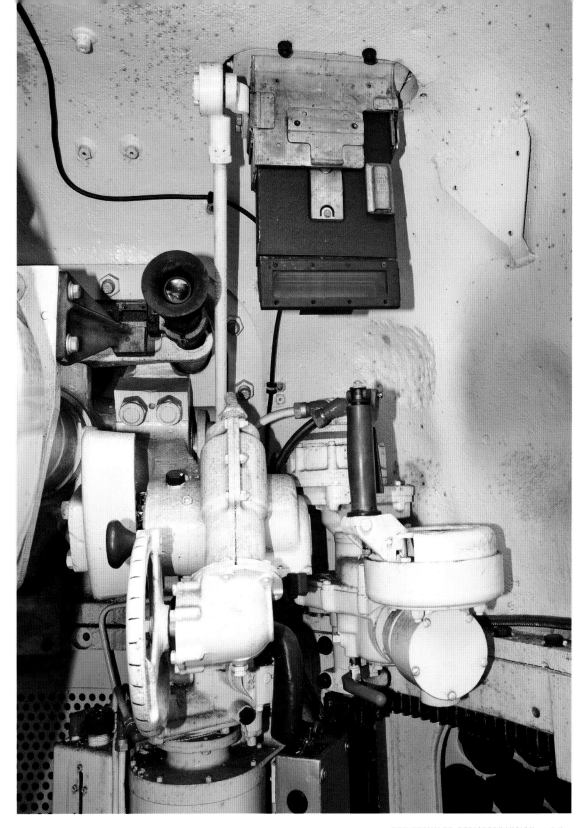

A view of the right front of the turret includes, *from top to bottom*, the gunner's telescope and periscope, the elevating and traversing handwheels, and the hydraulic traversing mechanism. *John Blackman*

As seen from the floor of the turret basket, to the left is the hydraulic traversing mechanism; at the center is the gunner's adjustable seat, above which, on the turret basket, is the turret-locking handwheel; and to the right is a stored Browning M2 HB .50-caliber machine gun receiver. Visible through the door in the turret basket is the right sponson, containing stored 75 mm ammunition and spare headlights. *John Blackman*

The breech ring, painted green, and the unpainted-steel breech block of the 75 mm gun are viewed from the right rear. The two threaded holes on the rear face of the breech ring are for extractor-plunger plugs, not installed. *John Blackman*

In a view from the left side of the turret basket, facing to the rear, the recoil guard of the 75 mm gun, *left*, partially hides the radio set in the turret basket. On the ceiling of the turret above the radio is a rack for storing .45-caliber ammunition clips. At the bottom are stored 75 mm ammunition rounds, and to the right is the inside of the Olive Drab pistol-port cover, with its operating handle attached to its upper left corner. *John Blackman*

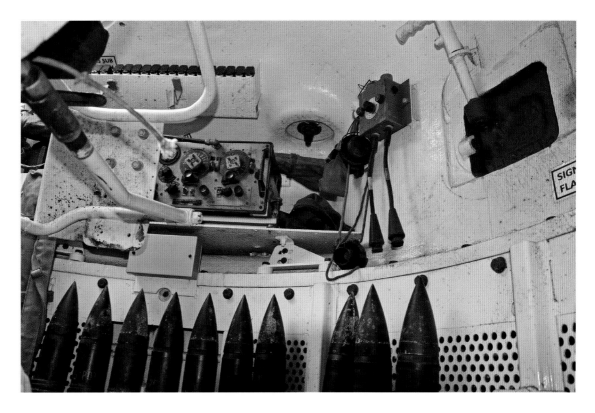

On the left side of the turret basket are 75 mm rounds, stored with their bases resting on cup-shaped holders and with clamps around the upper parts of the casings. Also present is the folding seat for the loader, shown in the lowered position. *John Blackman*

The grille/doors for engine-air intake are viewed from above the rear of the turret. On the outboard sides of the doors are armored covers for the fuel, engine oil, and coolant fillers. *John Blackman*

The left filler covers are shown close-up, including their locking pins, which are fitted with retainer chains. The cover for the diesel fuel filler is protected by a semicircular splash guard. To the right, behind another splash guard, are the hood for the fire-extinguisher pull handles, and the armored cover for the fuel tank filler for the auxiliary generator. *John Blackman*

Small-hatch Medium Tank M4A2, Ordnance number 15161 and registration number 3056341, assembled by the Federal Machine and Welder Company, Warren, Ohio, is shown during testing by the Ordnance Operation, Engineering Standards Vehicle Laboratory, Detroit, Michigan, on March 6, 1944. For improved protection, appliqué armor was welded onto the sides of the upper hull, adjacent to ammunition storage spaces, and on the fronts of the driver's and assistant driver's hoods. This turret is a model D50878, on which the right front face, previously a weak spot with thinner armor to provide clearance for the traversing gear, has been thickened; the horizontal ledge or overhang on this part of the turret, visible upon close inspection slightly above the top of the turret splash guard, is a visual identifier for turrets with the thickened armor. Sand skirts are installed; these sheet-metal structures seldom made it very far into combat zones before being damaged or discarded. An E8543 single-piece final-drive assembly is installed. *Patton Museum*

An M4A2, registration number 3056341, is observed from the right side. A very close inspection of the photo reveals three slightly raised weld beads between the glacis and the side of the upper hull. The two plates of appliqué armor have beveled weld beads around their tops and sides. The track-support rollers are mounted on spacers, also called pillow blocks, to raise them slightly above the roller support arms. *Patton Museum*

By now, in addition to the idler wrench, a sledgehammer was being stored on the rear vertical plate of the upper hull. Brackets were provided for the hammer head and handle, with a strap through a footman loop to hold the sledgehammer in place. Below the rear plate is an exhaust deflector, with a cutout for the exhausts, which is supported on each side by a piece of metal strapping (some deflectors would have closed sides). A folded tarpaulin is secured to the turret bustle with straps through footman loops. At this stage, the turret bustles lacked brackets for storing the .50-caliber antiaircraft machine gun. *Patton Museum*

This Federal Machine and Welder M4A2, registration number 3056341 and Ordnance number 15161, accepted in September 1943 and photographed on March 6, 1944, had appliqué armor plates welded to the fronts of the drivers' hoods. The hoods were a cast type. Several recently introduced features are visible, including the travel lock for the 75 mm gun on the glacis, the brush guards for the periscopes that are on rotating mounts (the guard for the driver's hatch periscope is not installed), the coil-spring equilibrators on the drivers' hatch doors, and the late-type vane sight to the front of the turret hatch. *Patton Museum*

The turret on this FMW M4A2 was the D50878 type with the pistol port on the left side deleted, since the Ordnance Department considered this port a vulnerable feature. A recently implemented feature seen on the edge of the roof of the turret is the aperture for a 2-inch smoke mortar, which was located inside the left side of the turret. The late-type vane sight is visible on the right side of the roof, to the front of the hatch. *Patton Museum*

A single appliqué armor plate was on the left sponson of this FMW M4A2. Interesting variations are present on the bogie assemblies. On the track-support roller arms of the front bogie unit, the raised lower rib has four small gussets cast in; this feature is lacking on the other two bogies. Also, the bogie brackets and the suspension arms display varying casting marks. *Patton Museum*

As seen in an overhead view of FMW M4A2 dated March 6, 1944, on the left side of the turret ventilator is a mount for a searchlight, a feature introduced in 1943. The 75 mm gun shield now lacks the two lifting eyes. Details are available of the drivers' hoods and hatch doors, including the padlock hasps under the grab handles, and the equilibrator springs, which assisted in the opening of the doors. *Patton Museum*

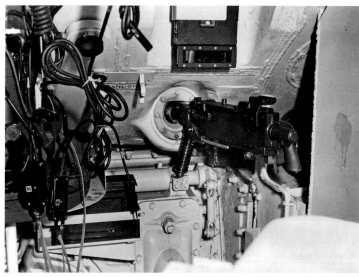

The same FMW M4A2 shown in the preceding March 1944 series, registration number 3056341, is featured in a photo taken on December 20, 1943, at the shop of the Ordnance Operation, Engineering Standards Vehicle Laboratory, Detroit, with the hatches open and a dustcover over the bow machine gun. In the foreground is a camouflage net, part of the on-vehicle equipment. *Patton Museum*

In the assistant driver's station in M4A2, registration number 3056341, at the top is the fixed M6 periscope, below which is the Browning .30-caliber M1919A4 bow machine gun, with a dark-colored equilibrator coil spring below the front end of the gun's receiver. To the lower left is the .30-caliber ammunition box and holder. *Patton Museum*

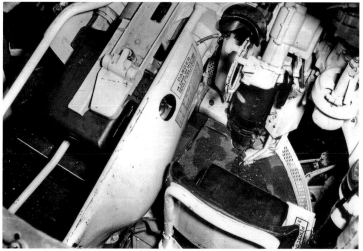

Identical in date and place to the preceding photo is a view of vacuum tubes, spare parts and accessories, and a pair of manuals for the SCR-528 radio set of the M4A2, which were noted at the time of the December 20, 1943 study, as having no stowage provisions inside the tank. *Patton Museum*

This is a vehicle commander's–eye view of the gunner's seat and controls and the 75 mm gun breech and recoil shield in the same FMW Medium Tank M4A2 portrayed in the preceding series of photos, on March 6, 1944. To the front of the seat are the elevating handwheel, the hydraulic traverse mechanism, and the manual traversing handle. *Patton Museum*

# CHAPTER 3
# Large Hatch, Dry Stowage

A decision was made in 1943 to significantly improve the Sherman's design while simplifying its construction. Henceforth all types of the Sherman, other than the M4A4, were constructed as large-hatch tanks. The small-hatch versions were manufactured by ten different plants, but large-hatch versions were made by only three factories: Chrysler Defense Arsenal, Fisher Tank Arsenal, and Pressed Steel Car Company. All three plants were already making Shermans when the large hatch was introduced incrementally, as will be detailed later.

A single, large plate now replaced the earlier multiple front-plate design. The new large plate was pitched at a 47-degree angle. Hatch bulges now were eliminated, and the hatches themselves were enlarged to make it easier to get into and out of the tank. In addition, a big ventilator was set in between the hatches in order to allow for the escape of gases generated by the firing of the weapons.

Internally, "wet" ammunition storage was a feature of most of the new tanks, with vehicles armed with 105 mm guns being the exception. The main-gun shells were stored in specially designed ammunition containers that featured fluid jackets that helped prevent ammunition fires. Large-hull tanks are therefore sometimes also called "wet-storage tanks." Since the small-hatch tanks lacked this type of ammunition storage feature, they are called "dry-storage" tanks. In fact, however, a few of the very early large-hatch tanks still incorporated dry ammunition stowage. These tanks will be discussed below.

Fisher Tank Arsenal was the producer of the large-hatch M4A2. This upgraded model of the M4A2 was turned out with both turret designs and with both the VVSS and the horizontal-volute suspension system (HVSS). By the time it ceased manufacture in the second quarter of 1945, Fisher Tank Arsenal had produced 3,100 M4A2 tanks.

The initial version of the large-hatch M4A2 was manufactured only with a 75 mm turret and VVSS suspension, and with no wet ammunition storage. An identifying feature of these tanks is the armor plates that were welded onto the side hull. The first of these Shermans were made under production order T-3608 by Fisher Tank Arsenal in the third quarter of 1943. Almost all the tanks produced under that order were small-hatch, periscope-hood M4A2 vehicles. The precise date that tanks of each type were built is unclear because Fisher Tank Arsenal made no distinction between the large-hatch and small-hatch Shermans within the production order. The lowest registration number that has been observed, however, is 3035813, a November 1943 production. Photographs taken during the war reveal that both small-hatch and large-hatch type tanks were supplied together to the USSR.

Output continued into 1944. A total of 2,389 dry-stowage tanks were manufactured under production order T-4340, which covered the period from February to May of that year.

Since the small-hatch M4A2 design included at least two major disadvantages, in its complexity of manufacturing and in the shot traps offered by the protruding drivers' hoods, a simplified design was devised during 1943: the large-hatch, dry-stowage hull. Fisher Tank Arsenal designed the production large-hatch hull and was the major producer of large-hatch M4A2(75)s and M4A2(76)s. Pressed Steel Car produced just twenty-one M4A2(76)s with horizontal-volute suspension systems in April and May 1945. Shown here is a Fisher-built M4A2, registration number 3035813, from November 1943 production. *Patton Museum*

Fisher M4A2(75), registration number 3035813, was a dry-stowage design, with appliqué armor on the sponsons. The exhaust deflector on the rear of the hull was the type with the closed-off sides. The D50878 turret had the single hatch with split doors (the so-called low bustle) and no pistol port. Because M4A2s with 76 mm-gun turrets came into production in May 1944, henceforth a distinction will be made between large-hatch vehicles with the 75 mm-gun turret, M4A2(75), and those with the 76 mm-gun turret, M4A2(76). *Patton Museum*

Medium Tank M4A2(75), Ordnance number 47564 and registration number 3080161, a large-hatch design, was completed by Fisher Tank in February 1944. It is seen from the front during evaluations by the Ordnance Operation, Engineering Standards Vehicle Laboratory, Detroit, on May 15, 1944. On the side and front of the bottom of the turret, to the rear of the assistant driver's hatch, is a dark area; this is a shadow, where the thickened armor in this area of the turret tapers off to a bevel. On the outboard side of the left headlight is the siren and its brush guard. *Patton Museum*

M4A2(75), registration number 3080161, had the final model of 75 mm gun turret: the D78461 turret, with a pistol port, a loader's hatch in addition to the right-hand hatch, and the so-called high bustle. Both the top and the bottom of this bustle were higher than on the D50878 low-bustle turret. On the center of the turret bustle depicted here is the trademark of the turret's manufacturer, American Steel Foundries' Cast Armor Plant, East Chicago, Indiana: a letter "C" inside an octagon.
*Patton Museum*

The side profile of the high bustle of the D78461 turret is seen to good advantage in this image of M4A2(75), registration number 3080161. On the rear of the turret bustle is an improvement: brackets for stowing the .50-caliber machine gun during travel. Note also the two equilibrator springs on the loader's hatch, and the travel lock under the barrel of the .50-caliber machine gun. *Patton Museum*

The support arms for the track-support rollers are the late, upturned type, which eliminated the need for installing spacers, or pillow blocks, between the rollers and the rears of the support arms. The upturned support arms, also referred to as track-support roller brackets, were designated part number C100823. *Patton Museum*

In a right-side view of M4A2(75), registration number 3080161, note how the roof of the D78461 turret to the rear of the right hatch has much less of a downward angle than on the "low-bustle" D50878 turret. *Patton Museum*

A final exterior view of M4A2(75), registration number 3080161, demonstrates the storage on the sponsons and the engine deck and also provides details of the turret and drivers' hatches. On the large-hatch hulls, the two ventilators outboard of the drivers' hatches were replaced by a single ventilator between the hatches. The round plate on the right side of the assistant driver's hatch was a cover for an antenna bracket. *Patton Museum*

The gunner's station in the turret of M4A2(75), registration number 3080161, is viewed from the rear. To the far left, atop the 75 mm gun, is a gunner's elevation quadrant, to the right of which is the eye cushion for the telescopic sight. The dark-colored instrument between the manual traversing handwheel and the turret-locking handle is an azimuth indicator, to give the gunner the precise angle of the 75 mm and coaxial guns with reference to the longitudinal centerline of the tank. On the wall of the turret are stored a wired-in flashlight, a binoculars case, the gunner's and commander's intercom control boxes, and, above the top intercom box, the commander's traverse override control handle, by which he could roughly bring the guns onto a target in terms of azimuth. *Patton Museum*

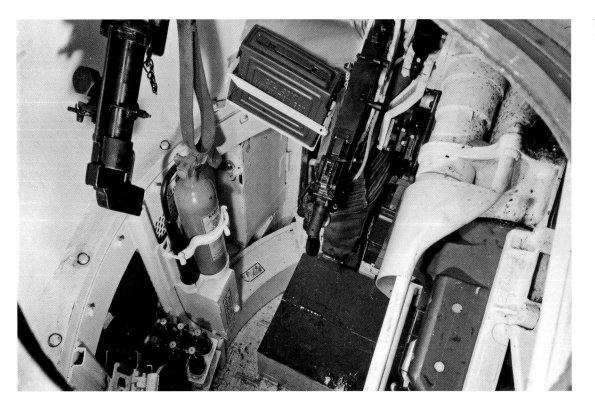

The loader's position in the left side of the turret is viewed through the loader's hatch in a photo from March 28, 1944. On the left are the 2-inch smoke mortar, a fire extinguisher, and six stored 2-inch smoke-mortar rounds. At the center is the .30-caliber coaxial machine gun, with its ammunition box to its left side. To the right are the 75 mm gun and its recoil guard. *Patton Museum*

Looking into the rear of the turret from the loader's hatch, to the left is the rear of the recoil guard of the 75 mm gun. At the top is the radio set in the turret bustle, below which are stored signal flags and a .45-caliber Thompson submachine gun. Three canteens are hanging from the bottom of the turret, while to the upper right is an intercom control box. *Patton Museum*

The lower left rear of the turret (the radio is at the top) and the rear of the turret basket are in view in M4A2(75), registration number 3080161. Secured to a bracket between the stored canteens is a Decontaminating Apparatus M2. *Patton Museum*

# CHAPTER 4

# Large Hatch, Wet Stowage VVSS 76 mm

The production of the Medium Tank M4A2(76), with its new turret armed with a 76 mm gun that was considerably more potent than the 75 mm M3 gun of the M4A2(75), began at Fisher Tank Arsenal, just as production of the M4A2(75) there was concluding. These large-hatch tanks were classified as wet stowage, meaning their 76 mm ammunition was stored in racks surrounded by a mixture of water and antifreeze, to prevent catastrophic explosion in the event one of the stored rounds was hit by enemy fire. This frontal view of M4A2(76), Ordnance number 47856 and registration number 3080453, was taken at the Ordnance Operation, General Motors Proving Ground, on June 10, 1944. From the start, the 76 mm turret featured a cupola with six vision blocks for the vehicle commander on the right side of the roof. The mantlet of this vehicle has its part number, E6180, on the top. *Patton Museum*

It was in May 1944 that Fisher Tank Arsenal began manufacture of large-hatch M4A2 tanks with a 76 mm gun. This production was carried out under an extension of production order T-4340, and the first tank to be accepted received registration number 3080441. This production order, which would run through May 1945, was the first of four wet-stowage orders under which 2,889 tanks would roll off assembly lines. These vehicles were made only as 76 mm gun tanks, but some had VVSS and others had HVSS suspensions.

In the end, this type of tank would be much more common than the large-hatch M4A2 with 75 mm guns. The turret into which the new, 76 mm gun was installed was a larger model, derived from the turret employed in the T23 Medium Tank program. Initial production models were fitted with the M1A1 76 mm gun with no muzzle brake.

Internally, wet ammunition stowage was the major modification incorporated into the Sherman at this time. While earlier tank models had ammunition racks in the hull sponsons—and as such were vulnerable even to minor penetrations of the armor—the new arrangement provided for the ammunition racks to be set in the hull floor and filled with a solution of water and antifreeze in order to reduce the risk of propellant fires in the event that the side of the hull was penetrated. In recognition of the larger gun and wet ammunition stowage, the designation of the new tank was changed to M4A2 (76)(W).

Virtually all these tanks were shipped off to the Soviet Union.

These photos of M4A2(76), registration number 3080453, were marked off in 1-foot grids, for dimensional reference. This left-side view shows the 76 mm gun lowered and resting in its travel lock. All iterations of the production 76 mm-gun turret had a pistol port on the left side and storage brackets for the .50-caliber machine gun on the rear of the turret bustle. *Patton Museum*

The cupola is visible in this right-side view of M4A2(76), registration number 3080453. The registration number is painted in small figures near the front of the sponson on each side of the tank. *Patton Museum*

Fisher Tank Arsenal M4A2(76), registration number 30116804 and Ordnance number 63782, with a wet-storage hull, was completed in October 1944 and appears here during tests by the Ordnance Operation, General Motors Proving Ground, on October 26, 1944. The 76 mm gun on this tank was equipped with a muzzle brake, which has a dustcover over it. A rearview mirror was mounted on each side of the glacis. The steel tracks are the T54E1 type, with chevron grousers. *Patton Museum*

M4A2(76), registration number 30116804, exhibits an exhaust deflector of grille design below the rear of the upper hull. Below the deflector is a tow pintle. To the sides of the pintle are double tow eyes, fitted with L-shaped pins with retainer chains. On the rear of the turret bustle is a feature installed partway through 76 mm turret production: an armored hood for a ventilator. Welded to the left side of the hood is a pintle for storing the .50-caliber machine gun. Jutting from the upper rear of the bustle are brackets for storing the .50-caliber machine gun barrel. A folding rack for storing baggage and equipment is on the vertical rear plate of the upper hull. *Patton Museum*

An overhead view of M4A2(76), Ordnance number 47856, provides details of one version of the D82081 turret. The cupola on the right side of the turret roof included a ring with six glass vision blocks; mounted on the ring was a hatch door with a round, slightly dome-shaped section on it that rotated on ball bearings and was equipped with a periscope. The left hatch was the same as the old commander's hatch on the M4A2(75), with split doors and a socket for a pintle for a .50-caliber machine gun on the hatch ring. *Patton Museum*

# CHAPTER 5
# A New Suspension System Is Introduced

The Fisher Tank Arsenal shifted production of its M4A2(76)s from vehicles with the vertical-volute suspension system (VVSS) to those with the horizontal-volute suspension system (HVSS) around the beginning of 1945. Some experts have estimated Fisher's production of M4A2(76)s with HVSS as approximately 1,300 examples, with the Red Army receiving around 460 of them under the Lend-Lease program. Canada bought some 300 M4A2(76)s with HVSS from the United States in 1946 and used them for training. Shown here is an M4A2(76) with HVSS, demonstrating the arrangement of three bogie assemblies on each side, each with two sets of dual bogie wheels, above which were two side-by-side horizontal-volute spring assemblies and a single shock absorber. The tracks are the T66 type.
*Patton Museum*

Introduced late in 1944, the HVSS with the 23-inch-wide track was soon worked into M4A2 manufacture. This suspension system, at times known as the E8 suspension, consisted of horizontal, rather than vertical, volute springs. Using the new HVSS system, dual wheels, and a much-wider track, the new tank boasted improved cross-country performance because ground pressure had been reduced from 14 to about 11 psi.

It is uncertain exactly when production began of the M4A2 with the HVSS, but this probably occurred shortly after the introduction of the new suspension system.

All M4A2 tanks with HVSS were fitted with the 7054366 turrets, which featured an oval loader's hatch.

Part number A7058424/A7058425, a two-section armored exhaust deflector, was another final feature of this version of the Sherman. This exhaust deflector assembly featured torsion rods at its base and could be folded into two halves. A hole in each of the small blocks located just below the luggage rack served to secure the deflector's halves when raised. This armored deflector made its debut in production in January 1945 and featured only on HVSS Shermans. The deflector was, however, also available as a modification kit.

The only combatant army to use the M4A2 (76) HVSS in World War II was the Soviet Red Army. A few of these tanks may have seen action against Germany in the final days of the war, but evidence for such use is scant. Photographic evidence does exist, however, for the use of these Shermans by the Soviets against the Japanese in Manchuria following the Soviet entry into the Pacific war on August 9, 1945, three days after the atomic bombing of Hiroshima. It is considered a possibility that Moscow set aside these Shermans specially for that purpose.

After the end of the war, the United States supplied Canada with M4A2 HVSS tanks in 1946, to replenish that country's diminished wartime armor. The tanks supplied to Canada had all the final production features mentioned above, plus a number of postwar improvements such as a first-aid box, an infantry interphone, and the armored exhaust deflector. Although it is sometimes thought that Canada employed these Shermans in the Korean War, in fact none of them saw action in that conflict. For logistical reasons, the tanks were reequipped with the M4A3 (76) HVSS.

The Pressed Steel Car Company completed 21 M4A2(76)s with HVSS during April and May 1945. The example shown here was equipped with the T80 tracks, with chevron grousers. The tracks were wider than those used on VVSS vehicles, necessitating fenders with supports alongside the sponsons. The serial number of the turret, 2752, is prominent on the side of the turret. Three spare track links are stored on the sponson.

| M4A2 General Data | | |
|---|---|---|
| Model | M4A2 | M4A2 (76) W |
| Weight, combat loaded | 70,200 lbs. | 69,400 lbs. |
| Length | 233 inches | 298 inches |
| Width | 103 inches | 105 inches |
| Height | 108 inches | 117 inches |
| Tread | 83 inches | 83 inches |
| Crew | 5 | 5 |
| Maximum speed | 25 mph | 25 mph |
| Fuel capacity | 148 gallons | 148 gallons |
| Range | 150 miles, approx. | 150 miles, approx. |
| Electrical | 24 volt negative ground | 24 volt negative ground |
| Transmission speeds | 5F | 5F |
| | 1R | 1R |
| Turning radius feet | 31 | 31 |

| Armament | | |
|---|---|---|
| Main | 75 mm M3 | 76 mm M1A1, M1A1C, or M1A2 |
| Secondary | 1 x .50 | 1 x .50 |
| Flexible | 2 x .30 | 2 x .30 |
| Ammunition stowage | | |
| Main | 97 | 71 |
| .50 caliber | 300 | 600 |
| .30 caliber | 4,750 | 6,250 |

| Engine | |
|---|---|
| Engine make/model | General Motors 6046 |
| Number of cylinders | 12 (two 6-cylinder engines) |
| Cubic inch displacement | 850 |
| Gross horsepower | 410 @ 2,900 rpm |
| Gross torque | 1,000 @ 1,400 rpm |

**Communication Equipment**

M4 Sherman vehicles were provided with SCR 508, SCR 528, or SCR 538 in the rear of the turret. Command tanks also had a sponson mounted SCR 506. All basic radios were provided with integral interphone.

Flag set M238 and panel set AP50A were also provided.

A Fisher Tank Arsenal M4A2(76) with HVSS, registration number 30122450 and Ordnance number 64471, is preserved on static display at the Kubinka Tank Museum, outside Moscow. The US Army accepted this vehicle during January 1945, before it was shipped to the Soviet Union under the Lend-Lease program. The T66 tracks are installed.

The travel lock of the M4A2(76) with HVSS at Kubinka is shown. When not in use, the upper part of the travel lock was secured against the vehicle by means of a latch on the glacis.

As seen from the rear, the vehicle still has the folding baggage rack in excellent condition on the rear of the hull, complete with brackets for storing the sections of a bore-cleaning staff. On the rear of the turret bustle, to the right of the ventilator hood, is the trademark of the turret's manufacturer, the Continental Foundry and Machine Company, Wheeling, West Virginia.

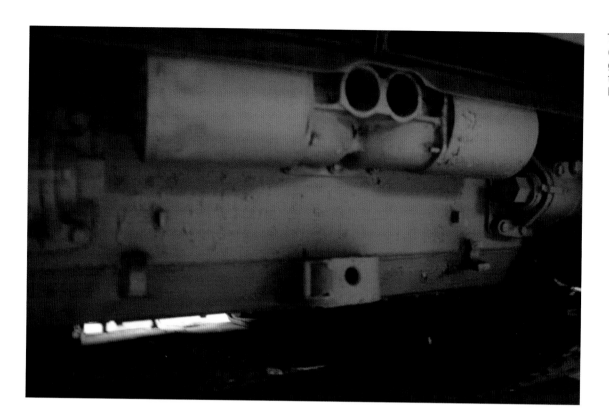

The mufflers with the cast-steel exhausts between them are in a good state of preservation. Below the exhausts is the mounting bracket for a tow pintle.

A closer view of the rear of the Kubinka M4A2(76) with HVSS shows details of the baggage rack, the right taillight and brush guard, the right-rear lifting eye, and the various brackets for storing pioneer tools. Between the taillight and the lifting eye is the cover plate for the compartment in the sponson for storing grousers for the tracks.

In a view of the engine deck from the left side, the cover for the left grouser box is missing. To the rear of that opening is a clamp for securing a tow cable. On the inboard side of the opening for the grouser box is the cylinder-shaped holder for the idler wrench.

The engine-air intake grille or doors on the Kubinka M4A2(76) with HVSS at Kubinka are observed from above its left side, with the armored cover for the engine-oil gauge to its rear.

Details of the left rear of the turret, the pistol port, the bolted-on splash guard below the turret bustle, and the four filler covers on the left sponson and the left side of the engine deck are displayed. Behind the turret splash guard are the filler cover for the auxiliary generator's fuel tank and the hood and pull handles for the fixed fire-extinguisher system.

On the right sponson and the right side of the engine deck, as seen from above, are brackets for pioneer tools, the left taillight and rear lifting eye, three filler covers, and, behind the turret splash guard, a ventilator cover.

From the upper right of the turret, features including the cupola, the two antenna brackets on the rear of the turret roof, the pedestal for the .50-caliber machine gun, the loader's hatch, and the loader's and gunner's periscopes are in view.

The cupola of the M4A2(76) with HVSS at Kubinka is seen from the front. At some point, the glass blocks around the cupola ring were painted over, and some of the paint is peeling off. Note the casting number on the frame of the hatch door, and the grab handle and periscope cover on the rotating dome part of the door. On the inboard side of the cupola is the travel lock for the .50-caliber machine gun. In the foreground, to the front of the cupola, is a setup pad, which was cast into the turret armor. When these pads were present on turret roofs, there were three of them, and they are believed to have been used for positioning the turret for machining.

This surviving M4A2(76) with HVSS has been painted and marked to replicate the markings of a famous Sherman unit of the Korean War nicknamed "RICE'S RED DEVILS," registration number 30114745. This M4A3E8 has a tiger's mouth and eyes painted on the bow. On the sponson below the turret is an armored first-aid box; these were introduced late in World War II. *Chris Hughes*

The air-intake grille/doors are open, as are the two-part, armored exhaust deflectors on the rear of the hull. These deflectors, which replaced the earlier, one-piece, sheet-metal deflectors, are supported by chains attached to small brackets on the hull. *Chris Hughes*

The two-piece exhaust deflectors are seen from the rear in the open position. Above the right fender is an infantry telephone, which allowed supporting infantrymen to talk directly and securely to the tank crew. *Chris Hughes*

The tracks on this M4A2E8 are T84s, a postwar model with rubber blocks with chevron grousers. *Chris Hughes*

The sprocket assemblies on the HVSS version of the M4A2(76) employed the same sprocket plates as those used on VVSS Shermans, but with wider drums to match the wider tracks. *Chris Hughes*

The idler wheels on the M4A2(76) with HVSS were dually mounted, with 22½-by-6¼-inch rubber tires. *Chris Hughes*

The left front bogie assembly is displayed. Each assembly included two dual wheels with 20½-by-6¼-inch rubber tires. Below the horizontal shock absorber on the top of the unit is the outboard horizontal-volute spring; an identical spring, but oriented in the opposite direction, is on the inboard side of this spring. *Chris Hughes*

The heavily worn T84 tracks are seen close-up as they bend around the right sprocket assembly. *Chris Hughes*

The folded-down baggage rack and the two-piece armored exhaust deflector in the raised position are viewed from the left rear of the restored replica of "RICE'S RED DEVILS." Note the hold-open brackets on the sides of the rack and the footman loops attached to it, for strapping down equipment. *Chris Hughes*

As seen from above the rear of the engine deck, the air-inlet grille/doors are open, revealing part of the engine compartment, including the four engine-oil filters on the forward bulkhead and two of the three air cleaners on each side of the power plant. Also in view is the bolted-down splash guard below the turret bustle, with its part number, C99378, cast on it. *Chris Hughes*

The engine compartment is viewed from above the right sponson, showing the two valve covers of the General Motors Model 6046 engine, between which are the two water-outlet manifolds and the exhaust manifolds. The three black-painted left air cleaners are at the top of the photo. To the left is the cover for accessing the engine-oil gauge. *Chris Hughes*

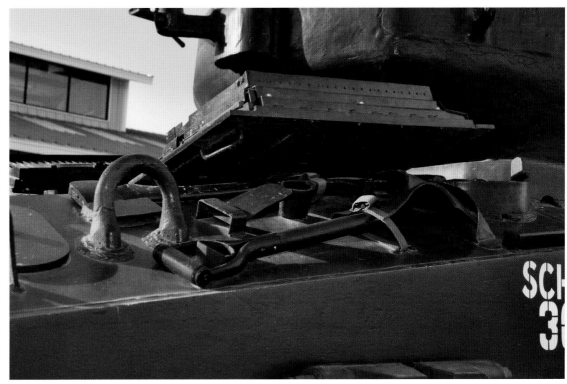

Secured to the sponson below the open right grille/door are a shovel, mattock head, and ax. To the left is the right rear lifting eye. *Chris Hughes*

In a rear view of the turret bustle, at the center is the armored hood for the ventilator. Brackets for storing a .50-caliber machine gun are welded to the ventilator hood and the upper rear corners of the turret bustle. On the top of the turret are two radio antenna bases and the pedestal for the .50-caliber machine gun. *Chris Hughes*

In a view of the roof of the turret from its front left corner, next to the loader's rotating periscope is the mount for a spotlight. A spotlight grip is inserted in the mount, but the housing for the light is missing. The disc with a retainer chain next to the spotlight mount is a cap that was placed on the mount when the spotlight was not installed. The travel lock for the .50-caliber machine gun is folded down next to the cupola. To the lower right, to the front of the setup pad, a faint circle indicates where an antenna bracket was filled in with a plug. *Chris Hughes*

The turret of the M4A2(76) with HVSS marked for "RICE'S RED DEVILS" is viewed from the right side. The lower part of the 76 mm turret was machined, either at a bevel that showed above the turret splash guard, as seen here, or only at the very bottom, so that it was mostly hidden by the splash guard. *Chris Hughes*

By the fall of 1944, a canvas dustcover for the 76 mm mantlet was in production. Such a cover is seen from the left side of the turret, with the metal retainers that secured it to the turret and the mantlet. *Chris Hughes*

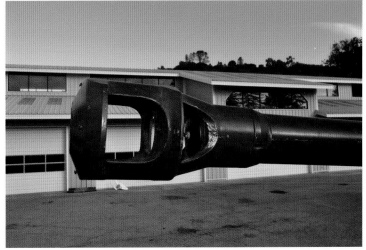

The left side of the turret displays a variety of textures as well as fairly rough machining around the lower part of the casting. Also in view are the pistol port and the left rear lifting ring. *Chris Hughes*

Early on, the 76 mm guns on the M4A2(76) lacked provisions for a muzzle brake. Then, barrels with the muzzle ends threaded for a brake were released, with the threads covered by a protective cuff. Finally, muzzle brakes became available and appeared on these tanks. The muzzle brake is viewed from the left side. *Chris Hughes*

Inside the left side of the 76 mm turret, the loader's revolving periscope is at the top, with the Browning .30-caliber M1919A4 coaxial machine gun and its ammunition box and spent-casings and links collector bags below it. To the right are the left side of the 76 mm gun breech and the recoil and carriage assembly to the front of it. *Chris Hughes*

The breech block of the 76 mm gun M1A2 of the M4A2(76) with HVSS is open, as seen from the left, showing the chamber of the gun. *Chris Hughes*

To the lower left, on the floor of the turret basket is a box with red-painted electrical foot switches for firing the coaxial machine gun and the 76 mm gun. To the front of this box is a foot pedal for manually firing the 76 mm gun in the event of electrical failure. At the center is the hydraulic traversing mechanism, with the box-shaped hydraulic reservoir on the left of the hydraulic traverse motor. The smaller cylinder on the bottom of that motor is the hydraulic pump for the stabilizer, which acted to keep the elevation of the 76 mm gun on target even as the tank maneuvered. To the upper right is the hydraulic traversing control handle. *Chris Hughes*

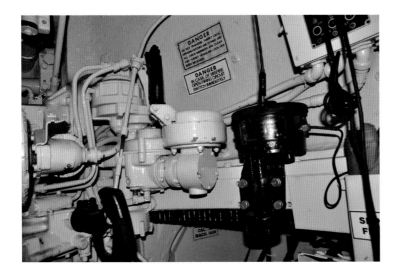

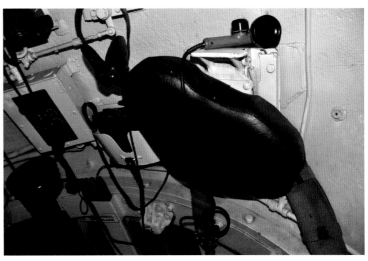

The upper elements of the hydraulic traversing mechanism are the focus of this photo of the turret, to the front of the gunner's seat. To the lower left is the control handle for the hydraulic-powered turret traverse. To the far left is the azimuth indicator. *Chris Hughes*

On the left side of the turret, the commander's seat is in the folded-down position. This seat was attached to the mount behind it and was height adjustable. Below the binoculars holder to the front of the seat are the turret lock and a signal-flag container. *Chris Hughes*

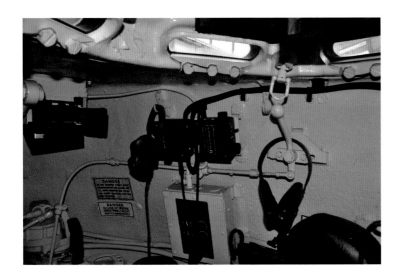

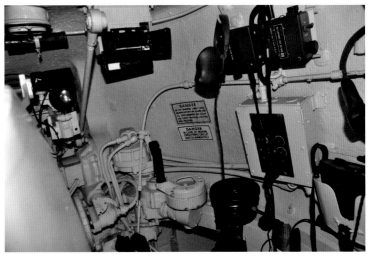

This is a view of the right side of the turret from above the recoil guard of the 76 mm gun. At the top is the lower part of the cupola, showing several of the glass vision blocks. The lever below the cupola to the left is the commander's traverse override control; using this control in conjunction with the vane sight on the roof of the turret, the commander could quickly slew the traverse of the turret roughly onto a target of his choosing. To the front of that lever is an intercom control box. To the left is the gunner's periscope. *Chris Hughes*

A final view of the interior of the turret of the M4A2(76) with HVSS incorporates the gunner's position, showing the telescopic sight to the left, the gunner's periscope with its mechanical link to the gun mount to the top, and the elevating and traversing mechanisms and the azimuth indicator toward the bottom. *Chris Hughes*

The following series of photos depicts the hull of a Fisher Tank Arsenal–produced M4A2(76) with HVSS that was extensively cut away to serve as an instructional chassis. It is on display at the Canadian War Museum in Ottawa, Ontario. The chassis is Ordnance number 65001, completed in March 1945. Seen here from the left rear is the engine compartment, with the GM model 6046 engine and its wiring and plumbing dominating the scene. To the right is the radiator, which too has been cut to show its cross section. All cutaway surfaces were painted orange so that trainees could see inside the engine and many accessories, such as the air cleaner to the left.

The engine compartment is viewed from another perspective to the left. To the right, painted orange, is the armor at the rear of the hull, while to the left is the forward bulkhead of the engine compartment, with armor cut away around the left sponson and the lower hull.

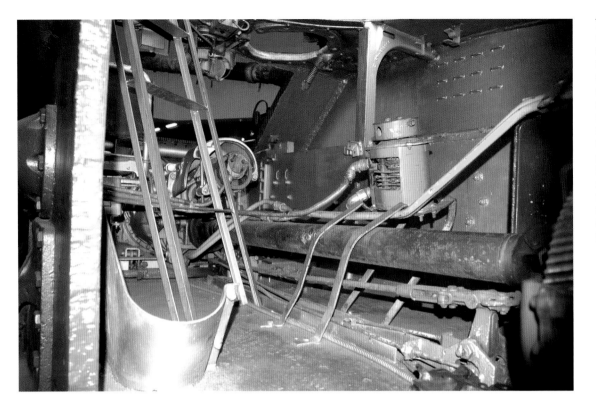

The fighting compartment is viewed from the left rear through an opening in the lower hull. The orange device above the driveshaft toward the right is the collector ring. It was on a rack for demonstration purposes; its normal location was on the turret-basket floor, and it provided the means for transmitting electrical power into the turret. To the left is a ladder installed for the use of instructors and students. In the background is the transmission, to the upper right of which is the assistant driver's hatch.

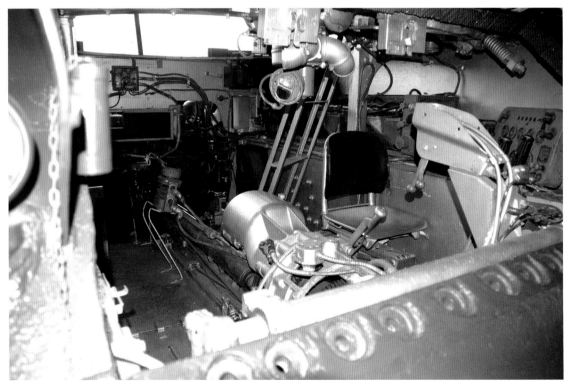

An opening cut through the glacis permits a view of the interior of the hull. In the foreground are the transmission and the driver's station, showing his seat, throttle controls, and instrument panel. At the top are the ventilator, the driver's periscope holder, and the equilibrator spring for the driver's hatch. In the background, the engine compartment is in view. Note that ammunition compartments are not installed in the bottom of the hull.

The final-drive assembly is cut away, showing the gears of the differential assembly in the center, to the sides of which are the steering brakes.

The left final-drive cover has been cut away to display its interior components. Also in view is the front left HVSS bogie assembly, including the flange by which it is bolted to the lower hull, and the two forward track-support roller assemblies.

# CHAPTER 6

# Field Use

Medium Tank M4A2, registration number 3020983, was one of six M4A2s that the Fisher Tank Arsenal delivered to the Desert Training Center, in the Mojave Desert of Southern California, for evaluations in February 1943. This tank was completed in July 1942 and had the initial type of suspension. Note that the suspension arms have gone flat from wear to the vertical-volute springs. *National Archives*

Most of the M4A2s that saw operational service did so with British or Commonwealth forces under the Lend-Lease program. In Commonwealth service, the M4A2 was known as the Sherman III. One such vehicle is being lifted by a crane mounted on a barge at Port Tewfik, Egypt, on September 9, 1942. A US Army registration number is faintly visible on the sponson. Note the damage to the rear of the sand shield, likely incurred during shipping. *Imperial War Museum*

Although the US Army received relatively few M4A2s, the US Marine Corps was equipped with large numbers of the tanks. The Corps first went into battle with M4A2s in the invasion of the Tarawa Atoll, on November 20–23, 1943. This tank, nicknamed "COLORADO," served with 3rd Platoon, Company C, I Corps Medium Tank Battalion, during the landings on the island of Betio in the atoll. The M4A2s of this unit had an elephant insignia above the nickname. *National Archives*

During the landings on Adelup Point, Guam, in July 1944, an M4A2 from the 3rd Marine Tank Battalion has become firmly mired in deep sand. This Sherman has appliqué armor on the turret but not to the fronts of the drivers' welded hoods. The object on the antenna bracket on the right side of the glacis is a canteen. The final-drive assembly is a Union Steel Castings type E4186. *National Archives*

A Medium Tank M4A2 from Company C, 3rd Marine Tank Battalion, has paused on the edge of a park at Agat Town, Guam, during the battle to take that island in July 1944. The number "8" is painted on the right side of the 75 mm gun's rotor shield, while a partially visible number or letter is painted on the other side. On the sponson is a white recognition star with white bars on the sides. *National Archives*

During the invasion of Saipan in July 1944, M4A2s of Company C, 4th Marine Tank Battalion, were fortified with improvised extra protection in the form of wooden planks attached at an interval away from the sponsons, with concrete packed in the interval, and with concrete troweled over the glacis. "Jenny" and "Lee 2nd" are painted on the fronts of the drivers' welded hoods. According to at least one source, the bucket-shaped object next to the turret hatch door was an improvised guard for the periscope on that door. *National Archives*

The plank armor, possibly with a thin layer of concrete sandwiched between it and the sponson, of this camouflage-painted Marine M4A2, nicknamed "EL TORO," on Guam on July 26, 1944, took several direct hits from a Japanese antitank gun. Nonetheless, these hits did not put the tank out of operation. Azimuth markings have been roughly painted around the bottom of the turret. The tactical sign of a number "1" in a triangle is on the turret and near the rear of the sponson. *National Archives*

At the tank depot at Chilwell, Nottingham, England, personnel, including women from the Auxiliary Territorial Service, are making adjustments to recently delivered M4A2s. The two closest tanks are Fisher Tank Arsenal–built M4A2s with the typical Fisher welded hoods for the drivers. The 75 mm guns are equipped with the early type of narrow rotor shields. T49 steel tracks are installed. *Imperial War Museum*

Members of No. 8 AFV Depot, Leicester, England, are performing maintenance and repairs on M4A2s before the D-Day invasion in 1944. A welder is making repairs to the right sand shield of the nearest tank, a Fisher Tank Arsenal M4A2, while the soldier in the foreground is cleaning the bore of the 75 mm gun. The presence of the siren on the left fender is associated with December 1942 to July 1943 M4A2 production. *Imperial War Museum*

The crew of a British army M4A2 stands by as officers of C Squadron, East Riding Yeomanry, confer on June 28, 1944. The distinctive, welded hoods for the drivers, a characteristic of Fisher Tank Depot M4A2s, are in view. A Browning M1919A4 .30-caliber machine gun is mounted on the turret hatch ring. The rotor shield is the D41288 type, with armored cheeks on the sides to better protect the point where the gun barrel enters the shield. Prominent casting marks are visible on the upper part of this rotor shield. *Imperial War Museum*

The Free French were users of the M4A2. Marshaled along a road in France during the Normandy Invasion are Shermans from the French 2nd Armored Division. The tank behind the one named "MURIENNE" is a Fisher Tank Depot small-hatch, dry-stowage M4A2 with welded hoods for the drivers; this tank is nicknamed "TARENTAISE." *Imperial War Museum*

A wounded Wehrmacht soldier passes a knocked-out Red Army M4A2 on the Eastern Front. The Sherman has appliqué armor on the sponsons, and a turret with a thickened right-front quarter. Both types of vane sights are installed on the turret roof. *Bundesarchiv*

"VALSERINE" is the nickname painted in large letters on the sponson of an M4A2 from the French 2nd Armored Division, seen moving through a village in France in 1944. This likely was very shortly after the tank landed in Normandy, since the designation of its assigned transport, LST-1119, is still chalked on he sponson. The drivers' hoods are cast on this example. *National Archives*

This knocked-out Soviet M4A2 with the turret blown off its mounting is the same tank seen along the road in the background of the preceding photo. Both tracks have spun off the suspension and are lying in front of the vehicle. The left grille/door on the engine deck also was blown open by the explosion. *Bundesarchiv*

German half-tracks roll past the Soviet M4A2 seen in preceding photos, alongside a road on the Eastern Front. The left grille/door was blown off, and the right grille/door is lying open. *Bundesarchiv*

A Soviet M4A2 with a strange log structure on its rear deck is lying partly in a ditch after being knocked out on the Eastern Front. A large number "39" is on the appliqué armor on the sponson. The left T49 track is partially dismounted. *Bundesarchiv*

Some M4A2s delivered to the US Army were employed for training tank crews, including these examples operating with a Medium Tank M3A1 at the Armored Force School, at Ft. Knox, Kentucky. The closest M4A2 bears the nickname "BEELZEBUB" on the sponson. *National Archives*

An M4A2 nicknamed "CHARLIE," from Company C, Medium Tank Company, II Corps Medium Tank Battalion, was knocked out during the Tarawa landing in November 1943. Several armor-piercing rounds, likely 47 mm, struck the sponson, with at least one piercing it and blowing a hole on the top of the sponson, next to the turret. A metal rack on the rear of the hull held eight 5-gallon liquid containers. *National Archives*

"COLORADO," a Fisher-built M4A2 commanded by Sgt. John R. Marn of Company C, I Corps Medium Tank Battalion, has paused next to Marine infantrymen on the beach on Betio during the Tarawa invasion. Visible on the right sponson are cleats that have been welded on to hold barbed wire, for repelling Japanese attempts to mount the vehicle. The tracks are the T54E1 type. *National Archives*

Marine crewmen of a Fisher Tank Arsenal–produced small-hatch, dry-stowage M4A2, with the early, narrow rotor shield for the 75 mm gun, pose for their photo during the battle for Saipan in the summer of 1944. An M1 helmet with camouflage cover is resting on the antenna bracket. *National Archives*

The Japanese registered a number of hits with 47 mm antitank projectiles on the turret and sponson of this Marine Corps M4A2, with at least three penetrating hits on the sponson. Even a relatively small round such as the 47 mm could wreak havoc on the crew and interior of a Sherman. Note the casting marks on the lower corner of the D68454 rotor shield. From a comparison with another photo, this tank can be identified as "COMMANDO," an M4A2 attached to Headquarters Section, I Corps Medium Tank Battalion. *National Archives*

Members of the 2nd Marine Division are advancing cautiously as an M4A2 accompanies them during the battle for Saipan, on July 7, 1944. The welded hoods for the driver are the distinctive, sharp-cornered units that were characteristic of Fisher Tank Arsenal M4A2s. Sandbags are on the top of the hull next to both drivers' hatches. Steel T54E1 tracks with chevron grousers are installed. *National Archives*

Crewmen of the 1st Marine Tank Battalion confer on their large-hatch M4A2(75), with "A7" painted on the front of the turret, at a recently captured Japanese airfield on Peleliu during September 1944. This was a dry-stowage Sherman, with appliqué armor on the sponsons, Note the track section secured to the turret for extra protection. *National Archives*

A Marine large-hatch, dry-storage M4A2(75) nicknamed "COMET" on the forward appliqué-armor panel and numbered "C22" on the turret is supporting infantrymen during the battle for Tinian in the latter part of July 1944. On the rear of the hull is the lower part of the exhaust trunk from the deepwater-fording kit. *National Archives*

While some of their fellow Marines labor in the incredible heat during the battle for Peleliu in September 1944, others have taken refuge in the scant shadow cast by a large-hatch, dry-stowage M4A2(75). The crew of this tank have a Browning M1919A4 .30-caliber machine gun instead of the usual .50-caliber machine gun on the hatch mount on the turret. *National Archives*

The Marine vehicle commander of a large-hatch, dry-stowage M4A2(75) is giving hand signals to the driver during a stop for replenishing ammunition, fuel, and provisions on Peleliu in September 1944. Three sections of T54E1 steel tracks are fastened to the glacis for extra protection from enemy antitank fire, while the tracks mounted on the tank's suspension are the slightly different T54E2 type. What appears to be "C7" is painted on the turret. The machine gun on the right hatch of the turret is a Browning M1919A4 .30-caliber. *National Archives*

A small-hatch, dry-storage M4A2 from the 3rd Marine Tank Battalion is disembarking from a landing craft on the black, volcanic-sand shore of Iwo Jima on February 24, 1945. Although the craft delivered the tank directly to the beach, the M4A2 was equipped with a deepwater-fording kit (including an unusual, drum-shaped air-intake trunk), and sealant covered the ventilators to keep out water. A star-and-bars identification device is on the turret roof. *National Archives*

Marines from Company A, 3rd Tank Battalion, eat their rations on and alongside a disabled, small-hatch, dry-stowage M4A2 nicknamed "ATEBALL," USMC registration number 72761, on Iwo Jima. Note the round adapter for a drum-shaped air-intake trunk on the engine deck. The appliqué armor appears to have been welded on in the field, judging from the way these plates have been freshly painted. *National Archives*

Marine Corps small-hatch, dry-stowage M4A2s from the 3rd Tank Battalion press forward on Iwo Jima in February 1945. The number "6" is on each side of the rotor shield on the lead tank, and "US MARINES" is written in block letters in a slight arc on the glacis of each tank. Star-and-bars identification signs are on the sponsons. The second Sherman has a radio antenna on the glacis antenna bracket as well as two on top of the turret bustle.
*National Archives*

During the battle for Iwo Jima in February 1945, a small-hatch, dry-stowage M4A2 with Company A, 3rd Tank Battalion, churns up volcanic dust as it speeds along a road toward the front. An indistinct nickname is on the appliqué armor on the sponson: some sources have identified it as "ATLAE," but it may actually have been "ATLAS."
*National Archives*

By the summer of 1944, Marines were going into battle armed with the new and improved large-hatch Medium Tank M4A2(75), such as this crew posing with their vehicle during the battle for Saipan in the summer of 1944. *National Archives*

A large-hatch, dry-stowage M4A2 nicknamed "GOLDBRICK JR." is providing support for Marines mopping up Japanese resistance close to Airfield Number "4" on Tinian in 1944. The USMC registration number, 100541, is between the appliqué armor plates; below that number is the UNIS (Unit Numerical Identification System), a half circle, representing the 4th Marine Division, and the number "133." *National Archives*

A large-hatch, dry-stowage M4A2 with two extra armor plates welded to the left sponson is employing an M1 bulldozer to knock down a shack during operations on Saipan in June 1944. Painted on the turret is "C.42." A battered lower section of a deepwater-fording exhaust trunk is on the rear of the vehicle. *National Archives*

This USMC large-hatch, dry-stowage M4A2(75) became swamped next to a Japanese barge when the left track went into a dip or shell hole off the shoreline during the landings on Saipan in June 1944. The intake and exhaust trunks of the deepwater-fording kit were installed. A nickname starting with the letter "G" is partly visible on the appliqué armor, indicating this probably was a Company G tank.
*National Archives*

During the battle for Peleliu in September 1944, a large-hatch, dry-stowage M4A2(75) assigned to Company C, 1st Marine Tank Battalion, is on the advance. Track sections are attached to the turret and the glacis for extra protection against antitank projectiles. The muzzle of the 2-inch smoke-grenade mortar is visible on the left corner of the roof of the turret. *National Archives*

The same M4A2(75) pictured in the preceding photo is viewed from the right rear as it advances during the struggle for Peleliu. The code "C9" is painted on the side of the turret bustle, and the split hatches on the turret are partially open. Five-gallon liquid containers are lying flat on the rear of the engine deck.
*National Archives*

Company B of the 1st Marine Tank Battalion served in the Okinawa Campaign. Seen here are three large-hatch, dry-stowage M4A2(75)s on the advance during that battle, on April 7, 1945. The first two vehicles have, respectively, "B1" and "B2" painted on the fronts of their turrets. As was often the case with 1st Marine Tank Battalion Shermans, three rows of track sections are on the glacis, and track sections are secured horizontally to the turrets. On the first tank, a few sandbags also are arrayed on the glacis.
*National Archives*

A Red Army M4A2(76) with fiberboard packing tubes for 76 mm ammunition stacked on the engine deck is standing by during the capture of Vienna in April 1945. Jutting from the rear of the turret is the vehicle's .50-caliber machine gun, with the canvas dustcover over it. The number "920" is painted on the side of the turret. Another Sherman is to the front of this tank.

A Soviet crewman relaxes next to the assistant driver's hatch of a large-hatch, dry-stowage M4A2(75) that has become stuck in a ditch, while the driver, standing in his hatch, watches to the left through binoculars. A tank jammed in this position will require a recovery vehicle to extricate it. *National Archives*